ADVENTURE AW

M000084902

EVERY BRAND HAS AN ORIGIN STORY.

OUR JOB IS TO HELP YOU CREATE YOURS.

WHAT WE'RE ABOUT

HELPING YOU LAUNCH STARTUPS SO YOU CAN ENJOY THE FREEDOM OF DOING SOMETHING THAT YOU'RE GOOD AT, INTERESTED IN, AND PASSIONATE ABOUT.

FINDING YOUR FLOW

*A TRAIL GUIDE TO HELP YOU FIGURE OUT
WHAT KIND OF STARTUP TO LAUNCH*

FINDING YOUR FLOW
A TRAIL GUIDE TO HELP YOU FIGURE OUT WHAT KIND OF STARTUP TO LAUNCH

Published by URTHTREK, LLC. www.urthtrek.com

URTHTREK, LLC
2034 NE 40th Ave. #414
Portland, OR 97212

urthtrek.com
@urthtrek

Manufactured in the United States of America.

ISBN: 978-0-578-24640-6

All photos and design are by the author. Copyediting by Frank Stirk.

CONTENTS

INTRO

WHY I WROTE THIS

I spend a lot of time with people whose lives are at a crossroads. "Should I go to left or right?" Unfortunately, there are usually a lot more decisions to make than simply which direction to take. These are weighty, anxiety-inducting decisions. Let me explain.

I spend my days with either university students in the classroom or with entrepreneurs in learning cohorts. The common denominator? Decisions. Which way to go?

Regardless of which topic I'm teaching in the classroom we inevitably end up talking about life. I see students I've spoken with who change their majors ... from nursing to digital media, from business to pre-med, from biology to social work. These are pivotal formative years where we settle on a life-trajectory. What we land on matters. They matter *a lot*. And so we fret. We process. We sort. We mull. We talk with others ... friends, family, professors, academic advisors, and more.

My role in this all? To help them process these questions and conversations. To also put their minds (and hearts) at ease. While we all begin life post-college on a certain trajectory it doesn't mean we're forever locked into it. We'll end up pivoting multiple times throughout our lives, even within the same profession or industry. But more than anything we talk about some of the subjects you'll soon be reading about in this book. Questions like ... who are you? Where did you come from? Where did you grow up? How did you grow up? What have been the shaping experiences or branching points along the way thus far? What are you passionate about? What needs do you see that break your heart? How do you want to make a positive impact for those who're on the margins or voiceless?

I ask a lot of these same questions in our learning cohorts. There are usually three different types of people who enter our cohorts with a desire to launch a startup: (1) those who've already started something but need help refining, focusing, and writing a business plan, (2) those who have a few ideas bouncing around in their imagination hoping to land on one during their cohort journey, and (3) those who have no idea what they even want to start.

Rest assured, all three are great places to be in. What I get to do with those who're either undecided or trying to pull an idea out of the air is to talk through and process these questions. You see, they're not as far off as they might think. Based on who they are, their past, experiences, temperament, interests, passions, hurts, and networks they actually already know some potential options of what to start. They need validation. They're not crazy. And ... they can do this.

Welcome to *Finding Your Flow*. I wrote this book to help you jumpstart the process. To already begin processing through what you want to start. Be encouraged. You're in a good place to be. Now, let's get started on this journey.

CHAPTER 1

ORIGIN STORIES

Oftentimes the best ideas come when least unexpected. For me it happened when I was on my bike. During the course of a typical week I'll ride three-to-five times. Sometimes these are laps around the local bike park here in Portland on my mountain bike. Most of the time I'm exploring the city on my gravel bike.

Bike rides are great opportunities for me to think and reflect. I am usually listening to a podcast or music. Guilty as charged as I ride through the city with earbuds in. Not too loud though so I can still hear traffic and when cars are coming up on me. Life is usually lived at a frenetic pace so a ride through the city is a chance to let my mind wander.

Many of my best ideas have come from the saddle of my bike. One example was launching my latest startup called URTHTREK. I had just sold my coffee roasting company. It was a five-year adventure of roasting coffee, selling coffee, scaling up, fine-tuning my message on social media, branding, networking, and more. It was a blast. So why did I sell it?

It definitely seemed like it was checking all the boxes I value … creative startup, outdoor-oriented for the target market, community development-focused, and so on. But something was missing. Over time I began to notice what really amped me up and what drained me.

In a non-typical manner, I'd write articles (or blogs) for our website. Who writes articles not even related to coffee for a coffee roasting company's website? Most often these articles were related to outdoors, adventures, exploring, mountain biking, trail advocacy, coffee brew methods, and so on. I love writing. I love it a lot. I realized I was much more energized when I wrote and had opportunities to speak and teach. Oh yeah, I forgot to mention: I'm also a professor. Teaching, researching, reading, and writing fuel me like little else. Tie that together with the outdoors, startups, community development, rural development, adventure, the creative economy, and post-industrialism creates an elixir that I simply cannot get enough of.

As I was reflecting on these while pedaling through Portland one day came the realization was that I needed to step more intentionally in this direction. My personal roadblock in terms of the coffee roasting company was that it didn't deliver me to my destination. I wanted to have direct focus on the outdoor industry, development work, and startups. By that point in my bike ride the ideas were swirling.

Over the last few years I had already begun mentoring startup entrepreneurs. I would gather them together in learning cohorts where we'd meet two times a month for a year. During that time, we'd explore topics such as vocation and calling, figuring out what to start, how to write a business plan, branding, marketing, and social media. It was and is life-giving. That checks these boxes of mine ... teaching, writing, startups, community development, and other related topics.

In rapid-fire succession it hit me … why don't I start something else that would allow me to continue to mentor startup entrepreneurs? But more than that, do so with a focus on the outdoor industry, community economic development, rural development, and adventure. To do what I've been doing all along, but this time more focused on a different market. By the time I had pedaled home the plan was already firming up. I must do this. There was no second-guessing, no hesitation. Instead of asking myself, "Why?" … I asked myself, "Why not?"

Thus, URTHTREK was born.

So while it may seem that I decided to start URTHTREK from scratch, just the opposite is true. URTHTREK really was and is a continuation of a thread that has been woven in me throughout my life. I just needed to see it.

What that means is that I didn't randomly grab an idea out of the air. It was the culmination (so far) of my life's experiences, interests and passions, my personality, and skills or talents. There's a cumulative effect. Experiences plus passions and interests plus personalities plus skills or talents lead us to where and how we land on a startup idea. I'll add one more in there … geography. Where you live matters and has an enormous shaping influence on your life.

So how did someone who was born and raised in rural Iowa get to the point of launching a company that focuses on mentoring entrepreneurs in the outdoor industry or artisan economy? I blame a P.E. credit in college for that …

It was my junior year in college in Nebraska and I had to fulfill one more P.E. credit for graduation requirements. I had one of two choices: bowling once a week for the semester or a three-day backpacking trip in Rocky Mountain National Park. I chose the latter.

As a kid who grew up in rural Iowa, a multi-day backpacking trip in the Rockies was a clarion call. The mountains were calling me. I listened.

We hiked twenty-six miles over three days and two nights. Everything was new to me and I was in awe. Elk wandered through our camp. I learned about pikas, why trees all of a sudden stopped growing at a certain elevation, and giardia. I got bonked because I blew through my food too fast and altitude sickness. I was hooked.

It was one of the best decisions I've made and it changed my life. It gave me a hunger and thirst for the outdoors that I didn't know I had. It also opened my eyes to life in the mountains, outdoor adventure, and even dipping my toes into learning more about the outdoor industry.

But what was it that compelled me to go backpacking in the first place? Why not bowling? I do love bowling. I was part of a bowling league as a child. Those were great memories and a lot of fun. So why didn't I simply opt to bowl? It's because two years earlier I blew out my ACL playing basketball. Huh?

I recall talking with the doctor about my reconstructed knee. He mentioned that a lot of the cartilage was damaged and had to be removed. As a result, he said that I should consider active sports that don't involve as much running due to the lack of a cushion on my knee from the missing cartilage.

That Christmas ... 1994 ... I decided to get a mountain bike. I vividly recall going to a bike shop with my Mom and picking out an entry-level mountain bike. Diamondback. $400. Fully rigid. Chromoly frame. Cantilever brakes. Black and purple. It was smokin' awesome.

Before I knew it, following my long road of rehab, I had connected with a couple of guys on campus who were mountain bikers. Since they were local they took me to some riding spots. I grew up riding bikes as a kid but this was my introduction to mountain biking. I was hooked.

I soon bought clipless pedals and practiced clipping and unclipping in an empty parking lot. That probably wasn't the brightest idea as I fell down over and over again. But I soon caught on. I kept riding. I rode a few times with one of my professors. It was that same professor who two years later would lead the backpacking trip to Colorado.

I read mountain bike and outdoor magazines. I soon started buying outdoor-oriented gear … from jackets to gloves to shoes and more. So by the time the opportunity came to go on this backpacking trip I was primed and ready to go. It was a no-brainer.

I hope you're beginning to see the thread that was being woven. By the time I graduated from college, I moved to Southeast Alaska for a season, then among other things worked as a hiking and mountain biking guide in Southern Arizona, attempted to launch an outdoor adventure non-profit in an immigrant and refugee neighborhood, started a mountain bike-oriented coffee roasting company, and now lead URTHTREK.

Looking back over more than twenty-five years it is evident that I didn't land on any startup idea out of the blue. Instead, each one followed a specific thread that had been there all along. I just needed to see it. That's what this guidebook is for ... to help you see the thread that's been woven into your life.

I am convinced you already have maybe five ideas swirling around in your imagination about what you could start. You simply need something or someone to help you process these different ideas. That's my goal for this short book ... to help you process.

What do you want to start? To you it may seem that your goal is far off or may even seem terrifying when in reality it may be a lot closer than you realize.

CHAPTER 2

INGREDIENTS OF AN ENTREPRENEUR

Hype is real. In the world of startups, entrepreneurialism, and even social entrepreneurialism there's an enormous amount of hype. Self-proclaimed entrepreneurs flaunt many different titles in their social media profiles, while others offer to help, support, and consult with entrepreneurs. If you're thinking of starting a business it can certainly be daunting. There are books to read, Facebook or Clubhouse groups to join, webinars, seminars, workshops, and conferences to attend (for a price), and so much more. Oh, and then there's the dress code. You know, you gotta "look" like an entrepreneur.

But does it have to seem that hard and so complicated?

I read an article recently about how new immigrants start more businesses than anyone else. Don't quote me on it, but you get the idea. Many of these entrepreneurs don't have websites or social media profiles. They simply start. Take our "tamale lady" as an example. There are many in Portland. We see them throughout our part of the city pulling a blue cooler on wheels shouting "tamales!" If I have the cash on hand I'll buy some because as a family we love them.

In the truest sense, our "tamale lady" is an entrepreneur. Would she self-identify as one? Probably not. I also have a hunch she's never read a book on entrepreneurship or startups nor attended any webinars. but she is what I'd call an "unintentional entrepreneur."

I think the crux of the problem is intimidation. We somehow think to be entrepreneurial we need to know the right language, be familiar with all of the books by all of authorities on the subject, and have sat through all of the webinars. By no means am I diminishing any of these resources as they are certainly helpful. I'm sure the tamale lady would benefit from learning about marketing and social media. The point is, most people who started businesses would never label themselves as "entrepreneurs" and yet they are working as hard as the self-proclaimed entrepreneurs to grow their business.

As a result, "entrepreneur" is one of those words shrouded in mystery. What is an entrepreneur? We immediately think of tech bros in skinny jeans sitting on therapy balls at their desks next to a ping-pong table somewhere in the Silicon Valley. Then there are all of the meet-ups and networking events we see or hear about in cities with young, driven, good-looking people getting ready to market their ideas. Is that what an entrepreneur is? If so, there's a reason why it draws some and repels others. But what in fact is an entrepreneur?

Simply put, an entrepreneur is "a person who creates and grows an enterprise."[1] The beauty of that definition is that while it certainly includes people launching a new iPhone app (and rightly so!) it also includes the young man in El Paso, Texas, starting a new riparian restoration non-profit or the young woman based out of Ogden, Utah who is venturing out to be a travel

---

[1] https://www.energizingentrepreneurs.org/content/chapter_3/tools/1_000027.pdf.

photographer. Interestingly, one in ten Americans are entrepreneurs. So maybe it's not all that mysterious after all. Nor is it an elitist endeavor.

With that said, what are the key ingredients of the entrepreneurial spirit? Regardless of whether one is launching a new coffee shop or a trail-building business there are certain essential ingredients. I came across them in the book *An Introduction to Community Development (2nd edition)* edited by Rhonda Phillips and Robert H. Pittman. Cultivating an entrepreneurial ecosystem is critical to the development of communities with a struggling economy. That's where and how this conversation is pertinent to URTHTREK and why it matters. It also is why we focus so much on startups and have learning cohorts.

In the chapter "Entrepreneurship as a Community Development Strategy," John Gruidl and Deborah Markley set forth these key ingredients. They write, "To better understand entrepreneurs, it is worthwhile examining the ingredients of the entrepreneurial spirit: creativity, innovation, motivation and capacity."[2] Let's unpack them …

CREATIVITY

Entrepreneurs may not be the ones who come up with an idea, but they are responsible for making it a reality. They make it happen. They market it. It is one thing to conceptualize an idea, but how will you breathe life into it? This is why entrepreneurs are creative. They're problem-solvers, they figure things out on

---

[2] Gruidl and Marklety, "Entrepreneurship as a Community Development Strategy," 280.

the fly. Ironically, most entrepreneurs are not even necessarily skilled in all the necessary areas when they start off, but learn along the way.

Starting something from scratch is a very creative process, regardless of what you're starting. How so? Because you're bringing something to life that did not exist previously. You begin with a blank canvas, and day by day, week by week, month by month, and year by year you paint the picture of what you envision your new business or non-profit will look like. Even if at the outset what you're starting doesn't seem all that creative, you still need the creativity to imagine something, to start it, and grow it.

INNOVATION

Along with creativity is innovation. "At the heart of the entrepreneurial process, entrepreneurs perceive opportunities and transform ideas into commercial products or civic services that people want and are willing to pay for."[3] Innovation involves taking an idea or process and adapting it and making it better. By definition, innovation means, "Make changes in something established, especially by introducing new methods, ideas, or products."[4]

You're not only a creator, you're an innovator. Again, both of those words can be a bit intimidating. We don't usually go around brandishing them. And yet as soon

---

[3] Ibid.

[4] https://www.lexico.com/en/definition/innovate.

as you start something you're innovating. Maybe you're tweaking an existing idea, bringing something brand-new into your community, or tackling a problem in a new way. That's innovation. During the entire life of your startup you'll continue to make changes along the way.

MOTIVATION

A common theme among entrepreneurs when it comes to motivation is this … p-a-s-s-i-o-n. It's not greed or vanity that motivates entrepreneurs. Instead, it's passion or a "I must do this" that's the driving force. That is one of the reasons behind the resiliency and adaptability of many entrepreneurs.

When we start something not only do we own it (both literally and figuratively), but in some ways it becomes an extension of our identity. It becomes a part of us We're motivated, excited, and passionate about what we're starting, the work it takes to get it off the ground, and to grow it. I don't know how to truly explain that sometimes raging fire within ... fueling us ... energizing us ... it's fun, crazy, and sometimes scary. I feel this way when I create new things, whether it's something like URTHTREK or even a new undergrad course that I'm constructing and teaching for the first time.

CAPACITY

"Successful entrepreneurs acquire the capacity they need to put their ideas into action."[5] Capacity could be either the space and margins in one's life that it takes to start and grow a business or non-profit ... and/or it has to do with expanding one's

---

[5] "Entrepreneurship as a Community Development Strategy," 281.

capacity as the startup grows. As I mentioned above, no one has all of the skills needed when starting out. They are acquired along the way.

I believe one of the marks of an entrepreneur is someone who can build capacity into their schedule. When I hear phrases like, "I don't have time ... I'm already doing enough ... I can't imagine starting something on top of what I'm doing," that tells me all I need to hear. Motivation plus passion plus "I have to do this" means most plucky entrepreneurs will simply make it happen. Get up an hour or two earlier, cut lesser things out of your schedule, work on weekends, and more. If you want to do this it will take sacrifice. That alone culls the herd.

These ingredients open the door to possibilities. Many would-be entrepreneurs fear starting down this path because they don't know everything nor have it all figured out. The reality is ... no one does. We're all figuring things out as we go. Be encouraged. If you're contemplating starting something you're in the right place.

CHAPTER 3

DETERMINING WHAT TO START

It's no cliché to point out that there are opportunities everywhere … because there really are. New businesses and non-profits are popping up every day. The larger the city the more we notice them, and that's simply the ones that are observable. There are even more that we never see because they're being run at home or from a coffee shop with a laptop computer. Others are on wheels … literally. I came across one of those yesterday.

I have been having issues with the dropper seat-post on my mountain bike. A couple days ago it finally gave up while I was riding laps at the local bike park in the city. I pressed the lever and dropped my saddle.

But when I pressed it again to raise it back up … nothing. It rebelled. Like a stubborn toddler, it refused to comply. I was powerless. No amount of coaxing or complaining or repetitively pressing the lever would convince my seat-post to rise back up.

Sure, I did several more laps (what else could I do?) and then pedaled home with my saddle all of the way dropped down. After I got home I debated taking it back to the bike shop that serviced it a month ago, but then I remembered that they actually had outsourced my brake and dropper post bleed job to a dude who runs a mobile bike shop out of his Sprinter van.

I DM'd him on Instagram, explained what was happening, and also that my lever had finally given out (which was the problem) as it bled oil in rebellion and angst. The next morning, I gave him a call, we chatted for a bit, and then set up a day for him to come and work on it. I knew I needed a new lever the last time my bike was in the shop.

Yesterday he drove up in his Sprinter van. The irony couldn't have been greater. There he was ... parked ... in the parking lot behind what was once my local bike shop. It had closed a couple years ago. With bike and camera in hand I went to meet him. (I had told him I'd be happy to take photos for him which I did.)

The whole process took maybe an hour, but I wasn't paying much attention. We talked, I watched, and snapped photos. I learned that he started his mobile bike shop earlier last year. He rattled off the other bike shops he had worked at before deciding to venture out on his own. I want to find out more about the origin of his business.

Something must've prompted him to eschew working in bike shops to go out on his own.

All of our startups have a story of origin.

There's so much more to the URTHTREK story than space allows. I've mentioned a few of the highlights and the thread woven throughout, but those are only some bits and pieces. The same goes for you. There's so much to your own story and journey that has been there all along. You simply did not notice.

One of the resources we use in our learning cohorts is the book *Born to Build: How to Build a Thriving Startup, A Winning Team, New Customers and Your Best Life Imaginable* by Jim Clifton and Sangeeta Badal. They provide a template … a framework … to help you process this very conversation. How do you know what to start? Again, that question may not be as daunting as you imagine. They write:

> Opportunities are everywhere. Extant literature on entrepreneurial cognition and psychology indicates that an individual's likelihood of recognizing opportunities increases with:
>
> a) prior knowledge of the environment (business, political or social)
> b) motivation to change the status quo (due to improvements in a process, new developments in regulations, technology or industry; or unexpected events of demographic shifts)
> c) the extent of their networks.
>
> Selecting the right idea to pursue may be the most important choice you'll make as a builder.[1]

---

[1] Clifton and Badal, *Born to Build*, 47.

Let's unpack this. As we do, my hope is that it will stimulate your own thinking and get your mind churning. Trust me, the answers are in there … we simply need to coax them out into the open. Ideas and dreams are that way, aren't they? They tend to be shy and reserved. Fragile. Kind of like finding a frightened and abandoned dog while driving through the backcountry. But with love, affection, time, and of course food the dog warms up to you and gains confidence and trust.

I will walk you through this quote as an exercise. I will continue to share more of my own story with you as well to give you an idea of what this process looks like in someone else's life. While hindsight is truly 20/20, I wish I had been more cognizant of these ideas and this framework earlier in my own journey. That certainly would've been helpful in steering me towards what I truly wanted and away from distractions and ideas that simply were not a good fit. Anyway let's jump in.

PRIOR KNOWLEDGE OF THE ENVIRONMENT

Landing on URTHTREK was not some random idea that came out of the blue. It actually was a continuation of a lifetime journey of moving in this direction. To be honest, when I decided to go for it I didn't even have all of the pieces in place nor was I even observant of them. However, I had enough to get me started. And the more I moved in this direction all those other pieces became apparent.

What was then my prior knowledge? Since my focus is helping those in the outdoor industry launch social enterprises (among others), part of my prior knowledge is having worked as a hiking and mountain biking guide, created a mountain bike-focused coffee roasting company, started previously multiple for- and non-profits, worked in higher education teaching (as I still do) in the areas of digital media, social media, community development, and entrepreneurship, and having already mentored startup entrepreneurs.

Am I suggesting that you need to know everything when you venture out to start something? No, not at all. You simply need to know enough. Everything else you'll learn it on the fly. Trust me when I say. We don't start off with all of the skills and knowledge we'll need from Day One. We pick things up as we go.

But to have a general knowledge or understanding of the industry and landscape you want to work in is essential.

Do you know the scene? The environment? Do you have a baseline understanding to get you started?

In the past year I've helped several new coffee roasters get started through our learning cohorts. Now, did each of these owners have prior and extensive knowledge of the coffee industry and coffee-roasting before they ventured out? Surprisingly, no ... not at all. Surprised? But they knew enough to get started. Some knew their community. Others knew their target audience incredibly well. Still others were masters at branding. The bottom line is none were previous roasters.

We all start somewhere. If we wait for mastery in whatever we're starting, or until we know everything about every area of our startup, we'll never start. I have a friend who's a part-owner of an outdoor apparel company. He shared with me how in a previous job he was hired for an executive-level role he wasn't even qualified for. He bought a book on what an MBA is exactly and how it works because all a sudden he had a slew of Ivy League-educated MBAs working for him. He didn't know until he knew. He had enough knowledge to land this executive-level job, but he still didn't know everything. You won't either. I certainly didn't ... and don't. Let's move onto the next point.

MOTIVATION TO CHANGE THE STATUS QUO

Are you a disruptor? Notice I didn't ask, "Are you angsty?" The term *disruptor* can be misused or misunderstood. The question you need to ask yourself is ... "What kinds of pain am I seeking to address or remedy with my startup?" In our cohorts we spend time talking about the pain points of your target audience. As soon as you have that figured out and begin communicating toward that end … pointing out these pain points, offering solutions, and empathizing with those who are suffering you'll find your reach growing.

What are you hoping your startup will change about your industry or environment? I'm not talking about macro issues, but micro ones that you can feasibly address or tackle yourself. Is it to make the outdoor industry more inclusive? To make mountain biking more ethnically diverse? To help the economic development of declining rural communities? To provide outdoor adventure opportunities to low-income families?

Every industry has a status quo. Somewhere deep within you is a desire to challenge or change it. That's what a disruptor does.

Before I decided to go full throttle with URTHTREK I was considering other opportunities. I was interviewing for an executive director role at an international non-profit. I happened to catch lunch with one of the board members who was in town for business. We talked about this opportunity and whether or not I'd be a good fit.

I'm a disruptor. I'm not angsty or angry. I just know I think differently from others and push back on the status quo. As I sat across the table from this board member I simply said, "I've finally come to the realization that I truly am a disruptor. What that means if you're interested in me is you need to know that I will want to change the status quo." I said that if they're looking for someone to simply manage what they have then I'm not the person they're looking for. However, if they want a creative thinker who will have uncomfortable conversations then I may be a good fit.

When I didn't get the job I was actually relieved. Although the board wanted change, the current staff and leadership did not. I would've stepped into a messy situation. Challenging the status quo was not what they ultimately wanted.

Do you want to change the status quo? If so, how? What does that look like for you? It could be a new innovation, a different way of addressing an injustice, a creative pathway for job creation in a declining rural community, a more inclusive rock climbing brand, and so much more. Don't shy away from this. Lean into it. Use your voice and platform.

THE EXTENT OF YOUR NETWORKS

Life is best lived in community. That is beneficial on both a personal as well as on a professional level. No one launches a startup in a people-less vacuum. The more robust your network the quicker the word spreads of your new startup. I've been a part of helping many entrepreneurs launch startups and I've seen a huge difference in outcomes between the person who goes at it mostly alone compared with those who have a community ... a network of people surrounding them, helping them, cheering them on, and spreading the word.

But it goes beyond that. Your community also helps you in recognizing opportunities. Maybe you're in a remote corner of your state or province. After you and your mountain-biking friends get off the trail, you talk about how to create more trails in your community. There are only a couple that you can ride. A local landowner has given you permission to build trails since they own thousands of acres of forest land. While you build and ride these trails they are only really accessible to you and a few friends who dig and build. What about others?

So you come up with a wild idea ... start your own trail-building company. Because you know a lot of people locally and regionally your business takes off ... in a hurry. You have relationships already with local, state, and federal agencies as well as numerous landowners. Pretty soon you're getting hired to build more trails throughout the region.

The point? Your networks matter. For some this part is easier than others. Also, the extent of your networks influences what you decide to start, but also its future growth. I've watched new coffee shops open, bikes shops take root, and co-working space get off the ground and I realized that the common denominator for those that took off in a hurry as ... networks. They are essential in getting your idea off the ground. They also can be key for access to funding.

This conversation lays the groundwork for the rest of the book. I mentioned earlier that you're not launching a startup in a people-less vacuum. Not only are you relationally connected, but your past, your experiences, talents and abilities, when combined with local needs, are all keys to helping you land on your startup idea as well as supplying the momentum to move forward.

For the remainder of the book we'll be exploring your path to opportunity recognition. What do I mean? "Instead of waiting around for opportunities to show up, let's discuss a process you can use to become alert and sensitive to unexpected events, to shifts in the market or customer needs, and to the possibilities that arise from the changing conditions around you. The steps to become alert to opportunities are:

1. Start with your talents
2. Connect the dots
3. Maximize your networks."[2]

Are you ready? Let's do this.

-----

[2] Ibid., 47-48.

CHAPTER 4

START WITH TALENTS

What are you good at? Seriously, answer it. Be honest. In order to do so you need to put away any sense of false humility. I'm not asking you to brag about yourself or to devolve into narcissism. Simple question … what are you good at?

If you're like me you have a hard time answering that. Call it insecurity. However, now that I'm closer to 50 than 40 years old, I am finally coming around to honestly answering this question. Why is it important? Because it is one of the keys to unlocking what you should start.

I had been wrestling hard with this question over the last year. In all honesty, it was one of the primary motivating factors as to why I sold my coffee-roasting company. While I could (and did) do it, what ultimately fueled me was not roasting coffee or scaling up the business. It was writing, teaching, photography, and social media. Even though we were a business, what excited me the most was writing articles for our website. I'd talk about adventures, exploring, how to drink coffee outside, and so on. That energized me like little else. I also grew to dread roast days.

In other words, I leaned into more about who I am, what I love, and the skills that I've learned (and continue to hone) along the way. I'm naturally curious and creative. Ironically, I started college as an art major. Yet because of a torn ACL during my second year everything shifted. I got serious about my studies. I love school ... learning, reading, writing, researching ...

and since then I have found a home in higher education. But that hasn't made me any less curious and creative.

I needed to admit this to myself and come to grips with it. I am who I am. I needed to build a career around my talents. So do you.

Clifton and Badal point out in *Born to Build*, "Pay attention to what you like to do and what you don't like to do. Remember, you're more than likely to be successful when you are using your natural talents because the opportunities you see and the solutions you build will be meaningful to you."[1] That's the key to uncovering what and how you want to start.

---

[1] Clifton and Badal, *Born to Build*, 48.

Sometimes in our learning cohorts there will be a couple of entrepreneurs who are starting the same thing. Right now I have two who are starting coffee roasting companies. Sounds simple enough, right? Just apply some cookie-cutter template and poof ... done. But no two entrepreneurs are wired the same. We as a cohort process how their personalities, backgrounds, skills and talents, and where they live, impact how they start.

One coffee roaster is very business-minded and talks of the nuances and intricacies of roasting coffee. The other is all about community and using coffee as a platform to build relationships and create a sense of belonging. Another is so cause-oriented that he's developing a plan to give away most of his profits to local causes. Just knowing that speaks volumes.

Here's a crazy question to think about … what if you could just be you when you launch your startup? That means recognizing what talents you bring to the table and then lean into them. While we can draw from the wisdom and experiences of others, there's only one you.

Clifton and Badal note that "to identify activities and situations that engage your talents, pay attention to these three clues: level of engagement, accelerated learning and superior performance."[2] These are personal assessments. Let's explore them more.

LEVEL OF ENGAGEMENT

> Have you ever been so immersed in an activity that you lose track of time? If you have, you were using your talents.

---

[2] Ibid.

Think about your experiences with a challenging exercise, a difficult project or a new hobby when you stretched yourself to the limit to achieve something difficult but worthwhile. If you were "in the zone"—a heightened sense of alertness, effortless performance, genuine satisfaction and immense enjoyment—you were in a state of flow. When you are in a state of flow, you are using your talents.

Building something is so challenging and will require so much effort that if you don't enjoy it, it will be hard to stay interested and committed. But when you apply your talents to an opportunity, you're more likely to be good at it—and that will give you the satisfaction, inspiration and stamina you will need to stick with it.[3]

Don't get me wrong. Creating and launching a startup from scratch is a lot of

---

[3] Ibid., 48-49.

work. A lot. But if it is something you're good at you'll find a deep sense of joy even in the midst of all of the work, including the long hours.

When a job is just a job, you look forward to "clocking out" and doing something else. But when you're starting something that's in the wheelhouse of what you're good at and passionate about it's on your mind constantly. You actually have to institute some disciplines so that you're not working on it around the clock. It can get messy for sure.

Where do you find your flow? Again, for me I realized it comprised teaching, writing, and creating. That doesn't mean they don't take a lot of work and effort. They do. Some tasks are definitely tedious, but I enjoy the overall process a lot. When that really hit home was when I came to the realization I needed to sell my coffee roasting company.

ACCELERATED LEARNING

> Think about the times in your life when you learned a new task, tried a new hobby or participated in an extracurricular activity. Now, think about the ones that you picked up and improved on quickly. When you learn an activity or task quicker than your peers do, you likely have an innate talent for it.[4]

Teaching at a private liberal arts university has its pros and cons, as does a large state university. At a bigger school you get to really hone in on your specialization and focus your studies on that. At a smaller school you tend to be more of a generalist even though you are able to dive into a number of specialties during a semester.

---

[4] Ibid., 49.

While my entry into higher education was teaching in the area of urban studies, since then I've branched out into all kind of fields from business to entrepreneurship to digital media to communications to religion and more. Believe it or not they're all interconnected.

I'm often asked to teach a new class. It could be a brand-new course that I have to build it from scratch or one that is simply new to me. I've come to realize how much I love this process. While I will have a baseline knowledge of the subject I get to dive deeper into it, read a lot of books, master the content, and then teach it. Since I now do this so frequently I've come to realize how much I enjoy it and how easy it is for me. Again, it doesn't mean that it's not a lot of work, but it comes together quickly.

This was another a-ha moment for me as to why I decided to launch URTHTREK and step away from coffee roasting. I love our learning cohorts, prepping and teaching, facilitating conversation, and continuously learning new things that make me a better leader each time I go through a cohort.

So what about you? As you read and process this, what things are you able to absorb and learn more quickly than others?

SUPERIOR PERFORMANCE

When have you naturally risen to the top? You may have noticed early success in writing or public speaking. Someone may have given you positive feedback about your musical ability or praised your performance in a sport. You might be good at organizing people or planning activities.

Look for opportunities in areas where your special abilities shine. You are

> more likely to achieve your goals when you are at your peak performance.[5]

This one is difficult to answer honestly if you tend to be more reserved or insecure. We don't want to go around boasting about our awesomeness. Listen, I'm not asking you to. This is just between the two of us. You're in a safe place. No one will accuse you of being arrogant. That said, when do you shine? In which areas do you rise to the top?

When it comes to higher education I find there are usually two main reasons why people become professors. (1) They are experts in their field. They are drawn in by the subject matter. Researching, writing, and discovering new things is what drives them. Spending time in the classroom? Well, not so much. You've probably had that kind of professor. (2) They love

---

[5] Ibid.

teaching and students. They're still experts in their field, but they also love and relish time in the classroom. For them, helping students to discover and learn is life-giving.

I'm definitely in that second category. I love students. I thoroughly enjoy and look forward to time in the classroom. I've worked hard to hone my craft, to become a better teacher, engage with students, and bring them into the discovery and learning process. Am I a master teacher? Time will tell. But I know how my students will rate me in their course evaluations.

As I noted earlier, I am finally coming to grips with what I'm actually pretty decent at. It doesn't mean that I've arrived. But I know what I can do and do well. Conversely, I know what I'm not much good at. When we line up what we're good at (and getting better at) with our startup up it elevates our chances for success as well as fulfillment.

That doesn't mean beginning a startup with 100 percent mastery of the business. There is still much to learn, but you know what? ... we're pretty good at it.

WRAPPING IT UP

These are the kinds of internal conversations I suggest you process and reflect on. It's all right to be honest with yourself. Identify what you're good at, what gives you life and energy. At the same time, be cognizant of what drains you, sucks the life out of you, and drags you down. Now you can see why you'll be so much more successful when you focus on what you're good at and brings you joy. There certainly is joy in mastery. Why would you not want your startup up to reflect who you are, what you're good at, and what gives you life?

Knowing who you are is not some cliché or abstraction. It is instrumental in determining not only what you should start, but how. The question I love asking entrepreneurs is this … what if you could simply be you in your startup? That's a great place to start. Besides, why would you not want to start there? There's only one you. Be you.

CHAPTER 5

CONNECT THE DOTS

"A sense of calling should precede a choice of job or career, and the main way to discover calling is along the line of what we are each created and gifted to be. Instead of, 'You are what you do,' calling says, 'Do what you are.'"[1]

At the beginning of my classes I like to share quotes. After reading the quote of the day we jump into discussing it. It's a way to get the conversation going. The authors I draw from range from naturalists to theologians, from activists to environmentalists, and from adventurers to entrepreneurs. Yesterday in class we

---

[1] Guinness, *The Call*, 45.

discussed the quote above from Os Guinness's book *The Call*. For a 9 AM class it was a fun and lively discussion.

College students are figuring things out on the fly. They switch majors, transfer schools, and usually work an assortment of jobs throughout their college tenure. Ultimately why they're in school is to get a degree— the proper credentials—to land a job after graduation that resonates with who they are, their values, purposes, and aspirations. In the midst of this journey of self-discovery we talk about vocation, calling, and figuring out what to do in life. And we wrestle.

I do my best to help them see the unbroken threads or story that is being woven or spoken into their lives. Even though they are young, there's enough already to reflect on as well as point them in the right direction. Part of it entails an awareness of these threads, their skills, personality, ambitions, and more.

I've personally had a difficult time seeing the threads that were being woven throughout my life which connected all of these disparate pieces. Either I simply didn't see or notice it, or maybe I felt I didn't have permission to do anything about it. When you step into any industry there seems to be a "right" way and a "wrong" way to do things. To go against the grain is to push back on the established collective wisdom … or so I thought.

There's perception and reality within every industry. Academic types are supposed to be this way. Lawyers are supposed to be that way. Whether you're a baker, tech executive, life coach, barista, accountant, or whatever … there appears to be a certain way to go about things that goes beyond procedures and processes. I'm talking about culture and identity. It's almost as if there's a preset personality or identity mold that you *must* fit into to. No exceptions allowed.

I grew up curious and creative. While I initially started my university studies as an art major I ended up switching degrees. In some ways it was as if I set aside the creative me to pursue these new ventures, opportunities, and openings. Besides, my new teachers and mentors didn't necessarily welcome or celebrate the "old me." It wasn't as if someone said outright that the curious and creative me wasn't acceptable. But the message did come through in more subtle ways. As a result, I moved away from that part of me.

But it never left me. Instead, it sat dormant for years. However, like magma inside a volcano that slowly pushes towards the surface under increasing pressure from deep in the earth, I could feel the pressure within me intensify. To keep from blowing my top like a volcano, I needed a release. And so I found one.

I explored. At that time we were living in Tucson, Arizona, and I got a job as a mountain biking guide. Since I was new to the area a whole new world opened up before me. New terrain, new history, new vistas, and all sorts of places to explore.

As a guide I had to immerse myself into not only the flora and fauna of the Sonoran Desert, but also its human history from the Hohokam (contemporaries of the more well-known Anasazi) to the Spanish missionaries who left an indelible mark on the region. I studied innumerable varieties of cacti, insects, geologic features, and more. In my free time I'd take people out on hikes. I would also load my family up in our beloved old Chevy Suburban with its 42-gallon gas tank and go exploring the region's high sub-alpine meadows and canyons and archaeological sites.

Something within me began to stir. At the time I didn't realize that I was beginning to connect the dots of who I am, my own story, my talents and abilities, and my longings. Before these were all random pieces, but now they started coming together. I'd be remiss to say that everything fell into place at once ... that I realized everything all of a sudden. I didn't. I still stumbled along. But I began noticing more that something with me was changing and I adjusted my life accordingly.

When it comes to deciding what to start, as I shared earlier, rarely, if at all, do we simply pull an idea out of thin air. Most often it's a continuation of a thread that has been woven into the tapestry of our lives. It may not be fully present throughout the entirety of our life, but certain aspects of it will be. In the course of our lives, we will continue to build on and expand our life experiences. These in turn become formative in determining who we are ... and what we start.

My torn ACL got me into mountain biking which opened my eyes to the outdoors which led to the backpacking trip which stirred my heart for the West, mountains, and outdoors. First in Alaska and then down to Arizona, I continued to hike, mountain bike, and explore. Eventually that landed me in the outdoor industry as a mountain biking guide. Even though most of our clients were affluent my heart was with those who didn't have the resources or know-how to venture out on their own. As a result, I moved into an immigrant and refugee community where I worked towards starting an outdoor adventure non-profit.

Since then there have been more pivotal life-changing experiences. And I am *still* connecting the dots. Life isn't linear. It more resembles riding a sailboat than a train. A sailboat is a lot more subject to the elements. A rogue wave comes along, or there's too much wind, or there's no wind, and a sailboat can get blown off-course.

"Research on human cognition suggests that builders [entrepreneurs] identify opportunities by making connections between seemingly unrelated events. Their ability to see patterns in disparate pieces of information and make sense of social, demographic, technological, policy or other changes happening around them leads them to ideas for new products and services."[2] Connecting the dots is about recognizing the patterns in your life ... the trends ... the trajectory.

Along the way we all make various starts and stops. As mentioned earlier, I see this on the university campus as students switch majors. I'm sure you did too. Once out of college many of us will make adjustments along the way. I have this conversation regularly with people who begin to orbit around URTHTREK. Usually it goes like this ... they have a career, a job, and even make great money. But they're empty inside. They want more. They tire of being a cog in the corporate machine. At the same time, they struggle because of the golden handcuffs ... their dependence on all the money they make. However, they also know

_____

[2] Clifton and Badal, *Born to Build*, 52.

that if they don't switch careers … and start something that is meaningful to them … they will feel like they'll wither away. I hear this storyline over and over again.

The good news is that your journey into considering a startup is not some blind endeavor. You're not coming at it completely from scratch. There are patterns, tendencies, and then of course desires in your life that move you in a certain direction. Intuitively you know it and feel it. Some things light your fires, but most often when you hear of or consider an idea, your normal response is, "No thanks." Why? Because it doesn't resonate with you. I can give you a list of ideas that I'd love someone to start, but I could also list a thousand times more other ideas that I have no interest in. I'm not good at that … I'm not wired that way … I have zero interest … zero ability … and I would die on the inside if I had to do it. The good news is that we don't have to do it.

What lights your fire? Take time to consider connecting the dots in your life. What patterns do you see? Jot them down. Talk to friends and loved ones. Process these conversations with others. Pay attention to what ideas stir up something within. You're already well on your way.

Are you ready to start? There is still one more component to consider …

CHAPTER 6

MAXIMIZE NETWORKS

A few weeks ago, I watched something amazing happen. There was a local event taking place. A pop-up. One of our former cohort participants was serving pourover coffees as well as selling t-shirts, whole bean coffee, mugs, and more. The coffee was amazing, the conversations were rich, and the pop-up a success. But what blew me away was watching Sam interact with people. I loved it.

It was only a little over a year ago that Sam joined one of our cohorts. He was thirty years old and had just recently moved to Portland. He had an itch to start up something but wasn't 100 percent sure what he wanted to start. However, a third of the way through the cohort he landed on an idea. Instead of waiting for the cohort to finish he launched his brand … Kids and Cobras. It's a moto lifestyle brand and coffee company.

Most of the time cohort participants live all over the place. Since we meet online and utilize video calls that doesn't matter. But Sam happened to live just a couple miles away from me. As a result, I've been able to attend several of his pop-up events, take photos, and enjoy watching him grow Kids and Cobras.

There are lots of reasons why some brands flourish and others don't. It could be due to finances or location or leadership, or maybe some other factor. It was only a few months ago that Sam started selling coffee. He bought a coffee roaster, learned to roast, refined his craft, and then began selling coffee. But watching him at the event, I realized that his success wasn't just because of the great branding (Kids and Cobras is phenomenal), or that he sold whole bean coffee in nifty cans that appeal to the moto culture, or the other swag he was selling. It was because of Sam's ability to network and be relational.

I watched him talk to everyone. And these weren't shallow conversations, they were meaningful. More than that, Sam had recruited an army of helpers and volunteers. As the day wore on I watched as he texted and called people out of the blue to come and help him. Sure enough, they did. But that's how Kids and Cobras started … in community. It was never a solo endeavor. From Day One, Sam had a network of people to share ideas with, dream with, and a crew who walked alongside him as he took the steps necessary to start and then grow his company. More than that, he continues to network widely in the moto world throughout Portland and beyond.

Sam demonstrated, without even realizing it, the final step required of figuring out what to start ... maximize your networks. "The next step in the opportunity recognition process is to talk to people in your social circle, especially those who are working in or are knowledgeable about your area of interest."[1] How often do we overlook this as part of our own discovery and startup process? I would've had to deal with fewer pitfalls if I had done this early on in my own journey.

Having a network of people is so important, especially as we're processing what to start

---

[1] Clifton and Badal, *Born to Build*, 55.

or do. While this doesn't pertain specifically to startups, I remember nearly twenty years ago being faced with a decision to step into a new leadership role. I was uncertain even though I wanted to do it. Fortunately I had a group of friends and peers with whom I could process this decision. They recognized that this new opportunity was a better fit for my gifts and abilities. They were so affirming that when I took on this new role, I felt energized like never before. It was a perfect fit.

While I probably could have made the leap without them, I needed to hear if they thought I was up for it or not. It altered my career trajectory. The best part for was that even after I started I was still able to tap into this network.

Going through this informal process of talking with the people in your network is a great way to evaluate what you're considering to start or do. We need people in our lives we can trust to tell us, "Hey, that's a great idea!" or "No, that's not you." We may not always get the answers we want, but it's important to be able to turn to people who have our best interests at heart to help us decide what to start.

Beyond that, the people in our network can help us get our startup off the ground. While they may not be there with funding and sweat equity, they can help spread the word, whether in person and on social media. It's kind of like having a group of Instagram influencers in your hip pocket spreading the good news of your startup, even if they only have 238 followers themselves. There is power when others share your story.

Lastly, include people in your social circle who can mentor you whether formally or informally. Think about all of the various aspects of a startup. There is branding, photography, social media, accounting, personnel, product design, sales, leasing space, and so much more. None of us can master all of these tasks. Having people in our lives who we can turn to for advice or wisdom is instrumental in our business's success and growth. This help can even come in the form of books or podcasts that give us valuable ideas and insights. These can be our "mentors from afar."

There are innumerable wise sayings and proverbs that speak to the notion of how it's better to tackle life in community. I don't need to list them all because I think you get the point. Whether you're the gregarious extrovert or the quiet introvert or fall somewhere in-between, we all need others around us to help us see things in life we might otherwise miss. When it comes to startups our relationships and networks are pivotal to the success of our venture. Who can you lean on? How can you tap into existing or new networks?

OUTRO

ASSESSING OPPORTUNITIES

Assessing opportunities is key in determining what we want to start. Also key is being flexible and adaptable. We may begin our journey in one direction but along the way there's a course correction. That's good. The truth is we wouldn't make the change unless we were already moving forward in the first place. We simply cannot wait until we have everything 100 percent figured out before we get started.

I've shared bits and pieces of my own journey thus far. There have been more twists and turns than space allows. That said, where I am today is because some of these course corrections. How did I ultimately land on URTHTREK?

URTHTREK started off as a mountain-bike guiding company. That was the plan. After having worked as a guide for others, I decided to try my hand at it myself. I created the business plan and began moving forward. But I needed capital. So I launched a crowdfunding campaign. I should've known better. Based on my previous fundraising experiences I already knew I was not very good at it. "Ah, but this time WILL be different," I thought to myself as I jumped in with both feet.

The plan was to raise enough funds to buy my own fleet of bikes, insurance, and all of the other funds needed to get it off the ground. I was eager, excited, and overly optimistic. I am going to do this! Well, no.

The campaign bombed. I didn't raise enough money to buy even a single mountain bike. I felt disappointed and sullen, and yet I had had a hunch from the get-go that because I'd failed before it would happen again. Now what?

Then a friend in L.A. reached out to me. He knew of a coffee roaster close to him who was doing private labels for anyone interested. Some companies were using it as a fundraiser. The roaster would roast, bag, and ship the coffee to the client. They'd split the profits 50/50. Well, that seemed easy enough.

I jumped at it. First, I needed a name, a logo, and a color palette. I had to design labels. I made one up on the spot and just went for it. Since I figured I'd need social media I created accounts. Before I knew it, I was off and running, trying to figure out how to sell coffee to mountain bikers. I had no intention of it being a coffee company. I just wanted to sell enough coffee to raise money to get the startup funds needed to get my guiding company off the ground.

But then something happened.

My idea worked. We started growing. Fast. Within a year we were featured in a couple of mountain-bike magazines and growing a following on social media. This was really gaining traction and momentum. I realized I had stumbled onto something. I decided to go for it. The guiding company would have to wait.

I bought a coffee roaster.

I learned to roast coffee.

I practiced and practiced for six months before severing ties with the roaster in L.A. They did a phenomenal job and I'm indebted to them. I simply needed to venture out on my own. Which I did.

One closed door led to one open door... and then another. That's how it works. Was I wrong to pivot? Should I have stayed the course and gone all-in with the guiding company? Did I sell myself short by switching to coffee? These are the type of questions that we all wrestle with. And we should. There's nothing wrong in that. But we cannot become paralyzed by indecision.

It's essential that we assess opportunities, figure out who we are and recognize our network. Somewhere in the midst of all of those disparate pieces lies the answer to what we want to start. And once we do start, we cannot be rigid. When companies become inflexible, they become like Blockbuster. It didn't pivot ... and Netflix took them down.

I'd like to leave you with this final quote from *Born to Build*. There are seven key questions you need to ask yourself as you assess the opportunities before you. Be honest with yourself.

> Vetting your idea(s) might lead you in new and different directions that you originally anticipated. Rarely do builders [entrepreneurs] start with a fully developed idea or know what their venture will ultimately look like.
>
> Opportunity recognition is an ongoing process. Be prepared to continuously refine and develop your ideas and fill your knowledge gaps as you adapt and adjust your goals. Be open to the process of exploration.
>
> To get started, ask yourself:
>
> 1. Why are you doing this? (Purpose)
> 2. What are you building? (Product / Service)

3. Who are your customers, and how are you helping them? (Customer needs)
4. What differentiates your product/ service from others in the market? (Value add)
5. What financial and social resources and skill sets do you bring to the table? (Resources)
6. How much are you willing to risk/ lose to make your idea a reality? (Affordable loss)
7. What does success look like? (Success)[1]

If you'd like help processing this I'd love for you to reach out to me at sean@urthtrek.com You can also DM me on the socials ... @urthtrek or on my personal account ... @seanbenesh. Thank you for joining me on this journey of discovery. I trust this was a helpful guide for you to read, think about, and reflect on. You got this. I'm cheering for you.

---

[1] Clifton and Badal, *Born to Build*, 57.

ABOUT

THE AUTHOR

Sean Benesh is a former hiking and mountain biking guide who currently works in higher education as well as mentors and coaches startup entrepreneurs.

URTHTREK

LEARNING COHORTS

What is a Cohort?

By definition, a cohort is "a group of people banded together." We also call them learning communities. In the context of URTHTREK, they are groups of entrepreneurs banded together on a learning journey to launch startups from scratch. Our role? Your guide.

Whether you want to journey through this with others in a learning community or as a solo endeavor we can accommodate both. Some prefer the one-on-one focus while others would rather have others with them. It's kind of like mountain biking or hiking (or insert favorite sport) where you can go at it alone and have a blast or explore with others. Both work.

Topics Covered in the Cohort

Who Are You?

It all begins with you. How do you launch a startup that is congruent with who you are? Your passions ... interests ... gifts and abilities ... personality. There are no cookie-cutter approaches. What if you could be you and launch a startup accordingly?

What Are You Going to Start?

Maybe you already know exactly what you want to start. Maybe you have a few ideas swirling through your imagination. Your time in the cohort will not only help bring clarity, but you'll fine-tune by refining your vision, mission, target audience, marketing plan, and more.

Why?

The "why" question is key. This is the double-bottom line conversation. How do you build generosity into the DNA of your startup from the very beginning? Make no doubt, you can be a highly successful business and seek the betterment of your community and others are the same time. It's not either/or, but both/and.

Structure of a Startup Cohort

Cohorts meet two times a month for an hour each time. We utilize Zoom for video calls so it doesn't matter where you live in the world as long as you have access to wifi or cellular data. For ongoing conversation we utilize Slack for communication for updates, announcements, and community building.

To learn more visit urthtrek.com or send an email to sean@urthtrek.com.

Made in the USA
Coppell, TX
09 August 2021

60236288R00069